TRINITY
COLLEGE LONDON

MUSICAL MOMENTS

Flute

Book 4

12 original
compositions
& arrangements
for Flute & Piano

Selected and edited by
Kirsty Hetherington

Piano accompaniment

Contents

Published by
Trinity College London

Registered Office:
89 Albert Embankment
London SE1 7TP UK

T +44 (0)20 7820 6100
F +44 (0)20 7820 6161
E music@trinitycollege.co.uk
www.trinitycollege.co.uk

Registered in the UK
Company no. 02683033
Charity no. 1014792

Copyright © 2011 Trinity College London
Second impression, March 2014

Layout: Catherine Duffy

Printed in England by Halstan, Amersham, Bucks.

The Call of the Angelus

arr. Robin Hagues

Albert E Walton
(died 1935)

3

Siciliano

2nd movement from Sonata no. 2 in E♭, BWV 1031

arr. Patrick Gundry-White

Johann Sebastian Bach
(1685–1750)

Sampan

Robert Ramskill
(born 1950)

Eine Träne

opus posthumous 70 no. 18 (1880)

arr. Patrick Gundry-White

Modest Mussorgsky
(1839-1881)

Eine Träne = A tear

11

Badinage

no. 1 of *Five Pieces* op. 56

arr. Jeremy Barlow

César Cui
(1835–1918)

The Banana Song

Mike Mower
(born 1958)

Along the Towpath

Christopher Gunning
(born 1944)

19

These Foolish Things

arr. Nicholas Hare

Jack Strachey
(1894-1972)

Carillon

4th movement from *L'Arlésienne Suite* no. 1

arr. Jeremy Barlow

Georges Bizet
(1838–1875)

Allegro

3rd movement from Sonata no. 1 'Fitzwilliam', HWV 377

arr. Patrick Gundry-White

George Frideric Handel
(1685-1759)

Mantas

Matt Smith
(born 1984)

Composer's note: This piece was written after swimming with Manta Rays. The flute represents the Mantas swooping in and out of view while the piano is the sea rippling calmly around them.

La Golondrina

arr. Paul McClure

Narciso Serradell
(1843-1910)

La Golondrina = The swallow

MUSICAL MOMENTS

Flute
Book 4

12 original
compositions
& arrangements
for Flute & Piano

Selected and edited by
Kirsty Hetherington

Published by
Trinity College London
Registered Office:
89 Albert Embankment
London SE1 7TP UK

T +44 (0)20 7820 6100
F +44 (0)20 7820 6161
E music@trinitycollege.co.uk
www.trinitycollege.co.uk

Registered in the UK
Company no. 02683033
Charity no. 1014792

Layout: Catherine Duffy

Printed in England by Halstan, Amersham, Bucks.

The Call of the Angelus

arr. Robin Hagues

Albert E Walton
(died 1935)

Siciliano

2nd movement from Sonata no. 2 in E♭, BWV 1031

arr. Patrick Gundry-White

Johann Sebastian Bach
(1685-1750)

Sampan

Robert Ramskill
(born 1950)

Eine Träne

opus posthumous 70 no. 18 (1880)

arr. Patrick Gundry-White

Modest Mussorgsky
(1839-1881)

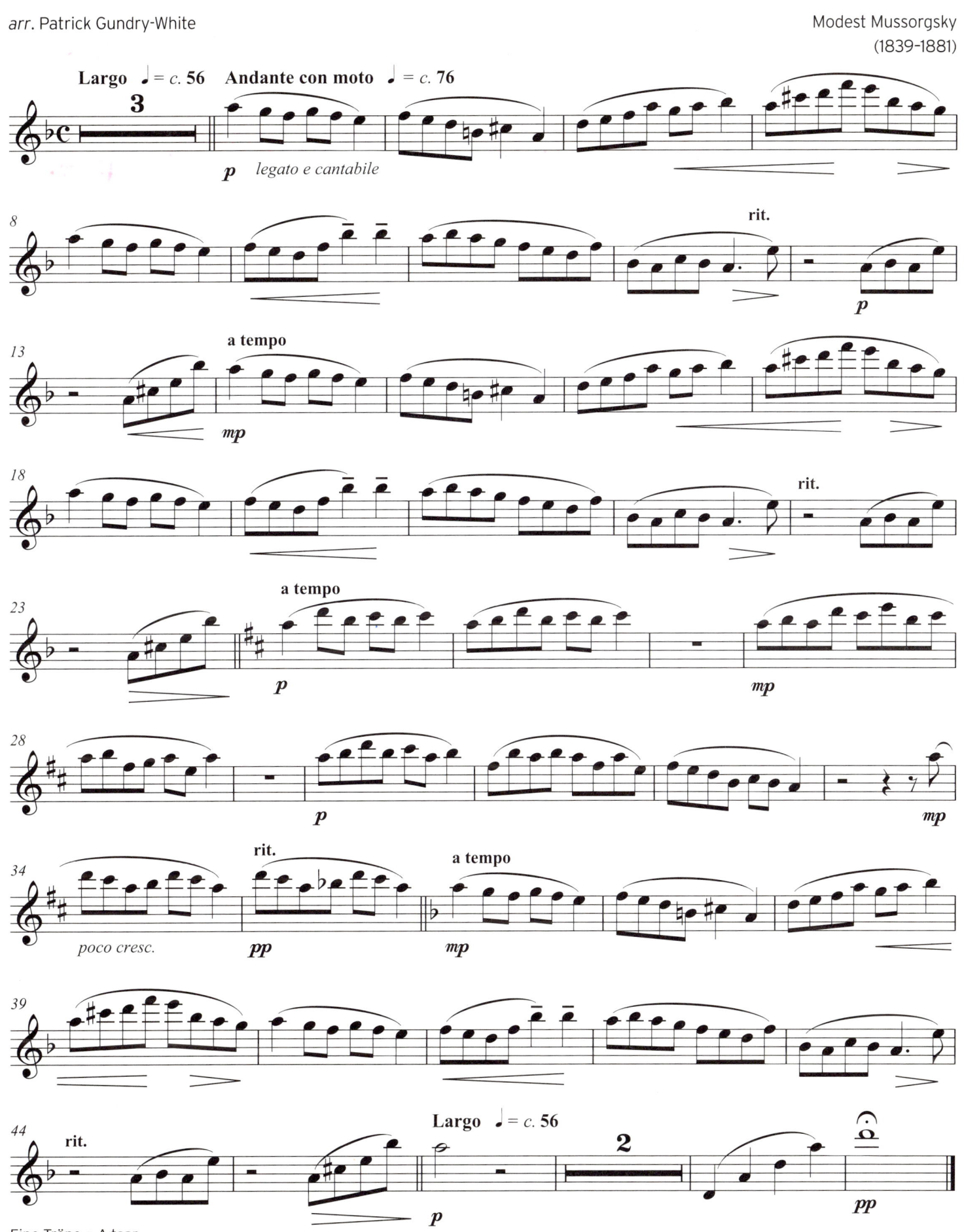

Eine Träne = A tear

Badinage

no. 1 of *Five Pieces* op. 56

arr. Jeremy Barlow

César Cui
(1835–1918)

Allegretto ♩ = c. 100

The Banana Song

Mike Mower
(born 1958)

Jazz waltz ♩ = 144

6

Along the Towpath

Christopher Gunning
(born 1944)

8

These Foolish Things

arr. Nicholas Hare

Jack Strachey
(1894-1972)

Carillon

4th movement from *L'Arlésienne Suite* no. 1

arr. Jeremy Barlow

Georges Bizet
(1838-1875)

Allegro

3rd movement from Sonata no. 1 'Fitzwilliam', HWV 377

arr. Patrick Gundry-White

George Frideric Handel
(1685-1759)

14th Oct.

Mantas

Matt Smith
(born 1984)

Composer's note: This piece was written after swimming with Manta Rays. The flute represents the Mantas swooping in and out of view while the piano is the sea rippling calmly around them.

La Golondrina

arr. Paul McClure

Narciso Serradell
(1843–1910)

La Golondrina = The swallow